A New Friend
The Story of Paul's Conversion

We are grateful to the following team of authors for their contributions to *God Loves Me*, a Bible story program for young children. This Bible story, one of a series of fifty-two, was written by Patricia L. Nederveld, managing editor for CRC Publications. Suggestions for using this book were developed by Sherry Ten Clay, training coordinator for CRC Publications and freelance author from Albuquerque, New Mexico. Yvonne Van Ee, an early childhood educator, served as project consultant and wrote *God Loves Me*, the program guide that accompanies this series of Bible storybooks.

Nederveld has served as a consultant to Title I early childhood programs in Colorado. She has extensive experience as a writer, teacher, and consultant for federally funded preschool, kindergarten, and early childhood programs in Colorado, Texas, Michigan, Florida, Missouri, and Washington, using the *High/Scope* Education Research Foundation curriculum. In addition to writing the *Bible Footprints* church curriculum for four- and five-year-olds, Nederveld edited the revised *Threes* curriculum and the first edition of preschool through second grade materials for the *LiFE* curriculum, all published by CRC Publications.

Ten Clay taught preschool for ten years in public schools in California, Missouri, and North Carolina and served as a Title IV preschool teacher consultant in Kansas City. For over twenty-five years she has served as a church preschool leader and also as a MOPS (Mothers of Preschoolers) volunteer. Ten Clay is coauthor of the preschool-kindergarten materials of the *LiFE* curriculum published by CRC Publications.

Van Ee is a professor and early childhood program advisor in the Education Department at Calvin College, Grand Rapids, Michigan. She has served as curriculum author and consultant for Christian Schools International and wrote the original *Story Hour* organization manual and curriculum materials for fours and fives.

Photo on page 5: Lori Adamski Peek/Tony Stone Images; photo on page 20: SuperStock.

Library of Congress Cataloging-in-Publication Data

Nederveld, Patricia L., 1944-
    A new friend: the story of Paul's conversion/Patricia L. Nederveld.
      p. cm. — (God loves me; bk. 48)
    Summary: Retells the Bible story in which Paul, on his way to arrest the followers of Jesus, sees a blinding light and is converted. Includes follow-up activities.
    ISBN 1-56212-317-3
    1. Paul, the Apostle, Saint—Conversion—Juvenile literature.
[1. Paul, the Apostle, Saint. 2. Bible stories—N.T.] I. Title. II. Series:
Nederveld, Patricia L., 1944- God loves me; bk. 48.
BS2506.5.N43 1998
226.6'09505—dc21
                                   98-16962
                                   CIP
                                   AC

10 9 8 7 6 5 4 3 2 1

A New Friend
The Story of Paul's Conversion

PATRICIA L. NEDERVELD

ILLUSTRATIONS BY PAUL STOUB

CRC Publications
Grand Rapids, Michigan

This is a story
from God's
book, the Bible.

It's for say name(s) of
your child(ren).
It's for me too!

Acts 9:1-20

"Hey! Let's put Jesus' friends in jail. They're causing too much trouble!

Now come with me," said Paul one day.
"Arrest them on the double!"

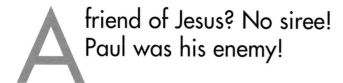

A friend of Jesus? No siree!
Paul was his enemy!

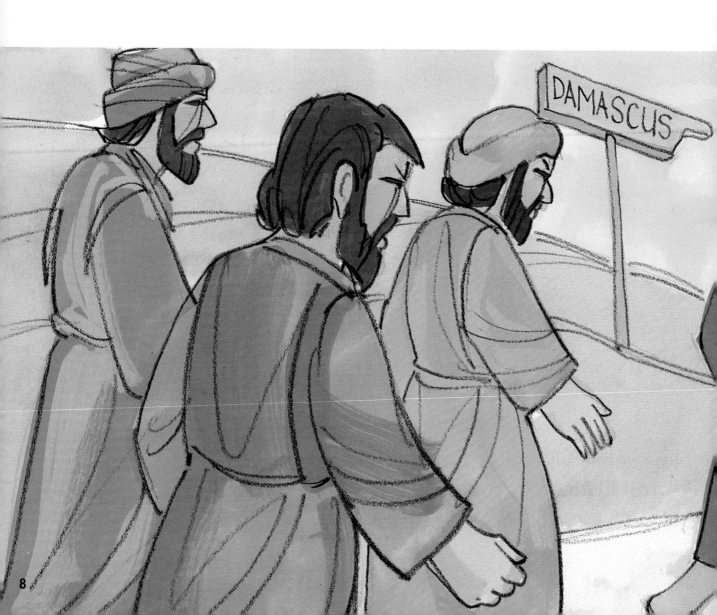

So to Damascus he did march
as angry as could be!

But on the way,
that very day,
there came a
blinding light.
It toppled Paul
right to the ground
and filled his heart
with fright!

There came a
voice that called
Paul's name:
"Why do you hate
me so?
Now please get up
and change your
plan!
I'm Jesus, don't
you know?"

When
Paul sat
up, he
could not see
his friends all
gathered 'round.
They took his
hand, they helped
him up,
and brought him
into town.

Then all alone,
Paul sat and
prayed
in darkness for
three whole days.
"Dear Jesus, I
don't hate you
now—
I'll be your friend
always."

So Jesus sent a friend to Paul to place his hands on him. Paul's eyes were healed—his heart was too! Now Paul was Jesus' friend.

"Dear Jesus,
you're my
greatest
friend.
I know just what
I'll do.
I'll tell all people
everywhere
that you sure love
them too!"

wonder if you know that Jesus is your greatest friend . . .

Dear Jesus, thank you for loving us so much. Help us to love you like Paul did. Amen.

Suggestions for Follow-up

Opening

As your little ones arrive, help them find friends who are already in the room. You may want to set out blocks, crayons and paper, or dress-up clothes. When you see children playing together, praise them for sharing with a friend.

Gather your little ones together and join hands to form a circle. Talk about how wonderful it is that friends can be together. Play a game of "Ring Around the Rosie" if you wish. As you sit down, tell the children that you're so happy to be their friend. Give thanks that Jesus is our friend too as you name each child.

Learning Through Play

Learning through play is the best way! The following activity suggestions are meant to help you provide props and experiences that will invite the children to play their way into the Scripture story and its simple truth. Try to provide plenty of time for the children to choose their own activities and to play individually. Use group activities sparingly—little ones learn most comfortably with a minimum of structure.

1. Provide flashlights and let the children enjoy shining them around the room, into corners, or onto their palms. Imagine with them what a bright light Paul must have seen. Older children may want to try a blindfold to experience the darkness like Paul did.

2. Using bright colored cardstock, copy the Jesus Is My Friend badge (see Pattern U, Patterns Section, God Loves Me program guide). Your little ones might enjoy coloring the badge with crayons or markers. Provide tiny heart stickers or scraps of colored paper and glue for adding decorations. Use a safety pin to pin the badge to each child's shirt. Children might want to make extras to give to a friend or sibling.

3. Invite your little ones to play "Follow Me to Damascus" as you retell the story. Encourage them to mimic your actions and facial expressions. Show Paul's angry face, look up as if seeing the bright light, fall down, cover your eyes, stand up and repeat with your children, "Jesus is my friend!"

4. Sing or say "Jesus Is a Friend of Mine" (Songs Section, God Loves Me program guide) as children mimic your actions:

   > Jesus is a friend of mine.
   > Praise him. (clap, clap)
   > Jesus is a friend of mine.
   > Praise him. clap, clap)
   > Praise him. (clap, clap)
   > Praise him. (clap, clap)
   > Jesus is a friend of mine.
   > Praise him. (clap, clap)

   Instead of clapping, you may want to use rhythm instruments, bells, or party horns or substitute other actions. Another option is to substitute the word love for praise. Cut out 3" (7 cm) hearts from red construction paper.

Make one heart for each child, and add short streamers for them to wave instead of clapping.

5. Cut out 5" (13 cm) hearts from pink or red construction paper or cardstock. Draw a happy face on the heart. Laminate or cover with clear contact paper if you wish. Then cut the heart from top to bottom to form two simple puzzle pieces. Invite your little ones to put the two pieces of the heart together, and remind them how happy Paul was when he became a friend of Jesus.

Closing

Encircle your group of little ones, and express your joy that Jesus is your friend and a friend of each of them. Say the prayer on page 21, then send each child home with a happy face sticker or heart stamp on their hand or cheek.

At Home

Your little one may just be discovering friends at church, in the neighborhood, or at a daycare center. You might want to collect photos of friends and family in a place where your little one can enjoy the pictures. Take time to look at the pictures together, naming each person. During prayer times, thank Jesus for each friend by name. Thank Jesus that he is your child's friend too.

Old Testament Stories

Blue and Green and Purple Too! *The Story of God's Colorful World*

It's a Noisy Place! *The Story of the First Creatures*

Adam and Eve *The Story of the First Man and Woman*

Take Good Care of My World! *The Story of Adam and Eve in the Garden*

A Very Sad Day *The Story of Adam and Eve's Disobedience*

A Rainy, Rainy Day *The Story of Noah*

Count the Stars! *The Story of God's Promise to Abraham and Sarah*

A Girl Named Rebekah *The Story of God's Answer to Abraham*

Two Coats for Joseph *The Story of Young Joseph*

Plenty to Eat *The Story of Joseph and His Brothers*

Safe in a Basket *The Story of Baby Moses*

I'll Do It! *The Story of Moses and the Burning Bush*

Safe at Last! *The Story of Moses and the Red Sea*

What Is It? *The Story of Manna in the Desert*

A Tall Wall *The Story of Jericho*

A Baby for Hannah *The Story of an Answered Prayer*

Samuel! Samuel! *The Story of God's Call to Samuel*

Lions and Bears! *The Story of David the Shepherd Boy*

David and the Giant *The Story of David and Goliath*

A Little Jar of Oil *The Story of Elisha and the Widow*

One, Two, Three, Four, Five, Six, Seven! *The Story of Elisha and Naaman*

A Big Fish Story *The Story of Jonah*

Lions, Lions! *The Story of Daniel*

New Testament Stories

Jesus Is Born! *The Story of Christmas*

Good News! *The Story of the Shepherds*

An Amazing Star! *The Story of the Wise Men*

Waiting, Waiting, Waiting! *The Story of Simeon and Anna*

Who Is This Child? *The Story of Jesus in the Temple*

Follow Me! *The Story of Jesus and His Twelve Helpers*

The Greatest Gift *The Story of Jesus and the Woman at the Well*

A Father's Wish *The Story of Jesus and a Little Boy*

Just Believe! *The Story of Jesus and a Little Girl*

Get Up and Walk! *The Story of Jesus and a Man Who Couldn't Walk*

A Little Lunch *The Story of Jesus and a Hungry Crowd*

A Scary Storm *The Story of Jesus and a Stormy Sea*

Thank You, Jesus! *The Story of Jesus and One Thankful Man*

A Wonderful Sight! *The Story of Jesus and a Man Who Couldn't See*

A Better Thing to Do *The Story of Jesus and Mary and Martha*

A Lost Lamb *The Story of the Good Shepherd*

Come to Me! *The Story of Jesus and the Children*

Have a Great Day! *The Story of Jesus and Zacchaeus*

I Love You, Jesus! *The Story of Mary's Gift to Jesus*

Hosanna! *The Story of Palm Sunday*

The Best Day Ever! *The Story of Easter*

Goodbye—for Now *The Story of Jesus' Return to Heaven*

A Prayer for Peter *The Story of Peter in Prison*

Sad Day, Happy Day! *The Story of Peter and Dorcas*

A New Friend *The Story of Paul's Conversion*

Over the Wall *The Story of Paul's Escape in a Basket*

A Song in the Night *The Story of Paul and Silas in Prison*

A Ride in the Night *The Story of Paul's Escape on Horseback*

The Shipwreck *The Story of Paul's Rescue at Sea*

Holiday Stories

Selected stories from the New Testament to help you celebrate the Christian year

Jesus Is Born! *The Story of Christmas*

Good News! *The Story of the Shepherds*

An Amazing Star! *The Story of the Wise Men*

Hosanna! *The Story of Palm Sunday*

The Best Day Ever! *The Story of Easter*

Goodbye—for Now *The Story of Jesus' Return to Heaven*

These fifty-two books are the heart of *God Loves Me*, a Bible story program designed for young children. Individual books (or the entire set) and the accompanying program guide *God Loves Me* are available from CRC Publications (1-800-333-8300).